UNDECEMBER
The Thirteenth Month

Amit Shankar Saha

Musca Press

Musca Press
an imprint of Culicidae Press®
PO Box 5069
Madison, WI 53705-5069
muscapress.com
editor@muscapress.com

Musca Press

UNDECEMBER: THE THIRTEENTH MONTH
Copyright © 2025 by Amit Shankar Saha
All rights reserved.

No part of this book may be reproduced in any form by any electronic or mechanized means (including photocopying, recording, or information storage and retrieval) without written permission, except in the case of brief quotations embodied in critical articles and reviews. For more information, please visit culicidaepress.com

ISBN: 978-1-68315-126-5

Library of Congress Control Number: 2025939746

Our books may be purchased in bulk for promotional, educational or business use. Please contact your local bookseller or the Culicidae Press Sales Department at +1-352-215-7558 or by email at sales@culicidaepress.com

culicidaepress.bsky.social – facebook.com/culicidaepress
threads.net/@culicidaepress – instagram.com/culicidaepress
x.com/culicidaepress

Design by polytekton © 2025

For Ananya

Table of Contents

Preface   7

Shukla Paksha — The First Fortnight and a Day   9
   Undecember   11
   The Enigma of Silence   13
   Cold Wind   15
   Footprints in Water   17
   Pictures   19
   Total Internal Reflection   21
   Mitigating Mathematics   23
   The Missing Tooth   25
   Denture   27
   Departure   29
   Grove   31
   Ecology of Love   33
   The Flavour of Missing   35
   Deep   37
   Missing You in Konark   39

Krishna Paksha — The Second Fortnight and a Day	**41**
Units of Forgetting	43
Your Side-bag	45
Waves	47
Wish Fulfillment	49
A Kaleidoscope	51
Telescope	53
Thereafter	55
A Slow Stirring Surface	57
Inconsequentiality	59
A Syntax Error	61
Rhododendrons	63
Silence of the Sleet	65
The World of Vestigial Organs	67
Gift	69
Morning Peace	71
Acknowledgements	**73**
Author Bio	**75**

Preface

A solar year consists of twelve months. But if a lunar year has to correspond to a solar year, then an extra month is required. This leap month is 'Undecember'.

My previous book was *Etesian::Barahmasi,* whose content was divided into the twelve months of the Hindu solar calendar and the section of each month had four poems totaling fortyeight poems. Many of my other poems could not find a place in that volume, and hence the advent of *Undecember: The Thirteenth Month* to accommodate the left-behind poems. This book represents a month of thirty days, divided into two sections: *Sukla Paksha* and *Krishna Paksha* – the Hindu demarcations for the waxing and waning phases of the moon – each comprising fifteen poems for the fifteen days of each phase.

These thirty poems convey the same ethos and sensibility of the previous book – being intensely personal and yet aesthetically accessible. The poems continue their play on *Sringara Rasa* of love and beauty mediated by the sense of *viraha*.

Shukla Paksha

The First Fortnight and a Day

1
Undecember

All throughout the year I steal
some days from dreamy weeks,
days post storms and cyclones,
when all is calm once again,
to build a thirteenth month
and name it Undecember,
a month, filled with days so light,
that it levitates out of sight.

In this invisible month
of stolen days all in red,
not found in calendars,
are moments when we met
to inhale each other's breath
until the truant winds swept
the seconds like dead leaves
into the dust of memories.

2
The Enigma of Silence

Words fail when sought.
At the stroke of utterance
I become as if muted
in a video call
by a technical glitch.

Silence stays in the network
of smiles saying so much
like an enigma.
Like the stars, like the trees,
unable to speak,

I wait for eloquence,
but the world intrudes.
and the moments fly,
like helium balloons
filled with rare potential.

In this phatic world,
drifting in vast silence,
we become part of that
surrounding universe
of expanding quietude.

3
Cold Wind

The cold wind reminds me of your coldness.
See how it enters the heart and freezes
the last vestige of warmth that memory
kept behind in the wake of your leaving.

The *shoka* of the old lover ferments
into the *dukkha* of the new poet
and the cold wind enters the poem too.
See how the words waver, pages flutter.

4
Footprints in Water

When we became as old
as the ancient peepal trees,
you passed thin like a reed
through the filaments of time,
and I searched your depths
to discover emptiness.

On the banks of Sarayu
you strolled alone the ghats,
while I came like a wisp,
whispering in the wind
the nothingness of space
and the birth of consciousness.

Far away in the night
when time crowds my room,
and memory becomes faint
while jostling for place,
breaths become conscious,
and longing leaves a trace.

When on the pristine banks
of the sacred Sarayu
you return to roam the ghats
and moor your mood somewhere,
you find me waiting like water
footprints left by your footsteps.

5
Pictures

When poetry came in pictures
you were a woman in red,
sometimes a spot of scarlet
amidst the green and the grey,
an indigo stream runs through the rocks,
pink and maroon monasteries,
white clouds climb up the brown hills,
virgin territory all...
and the children raising their hands,
posing for photographs
beside the lake, beside the trees
and the flags fluttering in the breeze,
my morning rolls up its sleeves,
and the tides of the night softly cease.

6
Total Internal Reflection

Having moved my eyes
    from you to me,
perhaps in a mirror
    I look to see
how do I look
    when I look at you.

Last night I raced
    the planets to know
how time is spent
    when I spend myself.

And last night I thought
    how time can stop
when I move my eyes
    from me to you.

And then there are days
    when I see in you
me and you in me
    and I don't know
what is this angle
    of co-incidence.

7
Mitigating Mathematics

Nights when I am in your city
I become breath and mix in the air.

Your empathy makes me palpable
like a soft breeze amongst the leaves.

Sometimes I feel that all the breeze
that blow on the earth are breaths of us.

The indifference of the planets
miss-match the hubris of lovers.

Sometimes I feel that sometimes I feel
else the world is barren of emotions.

Sometimes I feel how many sometimes
make millions and then eternity.

Sometimes I feel I am still learning
this mitigating mathematics.

8
The Missing Tooth

When I got my tooth extracted
something of my being got lost.
I am no longer the full me.
When I take a bite, some food
misses the grinding of the teeth.
The left cheek sometimes gets sucked in.
When I come to you I feel
myself as a lesser being,
who no longer deserves you.
Life has its ways to make us
realize that the body is
on its journey down the hill.
Our bodies have left their peaks
but the minds should not let go -
we know how dark is the path below.
The missing tooth speaks to me
of all those I am to lose,
leaving a hollow in my mouth.
In that hollow space of existence
there is just one desire left,
to hold on to you till the end.

9
Denture

Today I got an artificial tooth
in place of the tooth that was extracted

last year. Have to get used to this foreign
element in the mouth. I tell you this.

What sympathy will you have for my teeth,
the surface of which never had feelings?

Maybe their hard enamel will pierce
the hardness of your silent demeanour.

Whatever feels tangible in my mouth
is now amorphous in your reticence.

One day perhaps I will lose all my teeth
then perhaps silence will be the best speech.

Till then let us rinse our mouth verbally
for we always maintained oral hygiene.

10
Departure

tongue cuddles the tang
of left-behindness

taste buds bursting
tartaric *paapri chaat*

mouthful of sun-dipped
soothing mango slush

lost sight of you
in hurried departure

hugging sense of loss
fading like the day

and soft savings
from a leaving winter

with the blooming of
an intruding spring

11
Grove

What if two trees
love each other,
how would they express it
since they can't speak,
except when the storm
rattles their leaves?

What if two trees
want to elope,
how would they escape
into the grove,
except by making their own
by the dispersal of seeds?

What if we want
to become the trees,
how would we wait
for the storm to speak,
except when we hide
in the grove we create!

12
Ecology of Love

We were born separated
by the measure of time and space
like a bioregion divided
by political boundaries.

We grew up as two countries
competing to increase
our carbon footprints
although our climate was one.

But fossil-fuelled love combusts
and becomes just carbon dust.
This burnt world is an infatuation;
it has not progressed underneath.

Love may be as naked as nature
and as still as the trees.
You may not see it progress
although its roots run deep.

13
The Flavour of Missing

At the end of the day
when I am on a train
I try to write a poem
about our missed meeting.

When I look out into the dark

I think

How beautiful is the dark
because in the dark I can
imagine that you are there
just that I can't see you.

As if the dark fields beyond
the train window are dark
because I miss you.

I know how the space of missing
gets stretched when the train takes me far.

It bubbles up like a metaphor
for estrangement in time and space.

Under Doppler Effect
longings shift relatively.

And this keeps us alive for the future.

14
Deep

Autumn colours of Daringbadi
roll over hills and clouds.

The sunset point looks charming
at dusk with you on the foreground.

The emerald trees ambush you
in a picture perfect moment.

At a bend on the country road
you jump with your arms spread,

a frozen frame where your feet fly,
as if you have levitated.

So happy to see you happy,
I say, before you go to sleep.

Morning brings these lines to me,
as if, I was there, somewhere deep.

15
Missing You in Konark

Last morning I told you
about my solo visit to
the Sun Temple in Konark.

Have you seen its wheels
that have traversed so much
distance in the space of time?

Someone promised to bring
the forgotten scent of rain
when it's time to meet again.

In the evening I went to
the Chandrabhaga sea beach
to hear the sound of the waves.

See how these lines roll and strike
the shores of this morning
and listening becomes longing.

Krishna Paksha

The Second Fortnight and a Day

16
Units of Forgetting

From the speeding train
the far light is moving
slow like a memory
that fades but fails to go.

In the night sky remain
constant the rolled out
eyes of the galaxies
whose twinkles don't die.

From those far distances
this speed of the train
is not even a blink
in the eye of time.

Everything is static,
nights after nights,
until we come real close
to notice the movement.

Sometimes I feel
how wonderful it is
that distance freezes
time like a chunk of ice.

But then the ice melts,
the distance deceives,
and changes are measured
in the units of forgetting.

17
Your Side-bag

I keep your side-bag
beside my pillow
on the bed,
so that I see it first
when I wake up.

Sometimes I
hug it to sleep.

On its body
of faded whiteness
in calligraphic French
is printed "Le nautisme" -
aquatic sports.

And in red and blue
little images
of boats, anchors,
airtubes, seabirds
and lighthouses.

Its zipper does not work.

You discarded it
and asked me to
throw it away
but also said that
you know I will not.

I have kept it.

18
Waves

At night waves of words come
from the shores of your books,
all frothing in meanings
with the foam of feelings.

I scoop up an ocean
in the cup of my mind,
you can hear the lapping
on the sands of my being.

Early in the morning
when I wake up I find
in the waves of my dreams
our wavelengths were one.

19
Wish Fulfillment

Today when you read your poems and I am far away

the rains will bend their direction to mourn the distance,

the lights will sit heavy on the evening of remembrance,

a lake in Kashmir will abruptly freeze in sorrow,

a mirage in Kutch will waylay a traveler for water,

memory will weave a flower patterned chintz curtain,

the dreams of the curtain will cover the world like a storm,

a poet will squeeze the universe in his palms and say,

"Today when you read your poems and I am far away

I wish the words that escape your lips all come my way."

20
A Kaleidoscope

A scolding begets a poem between us
while the seasons change to birth a flu.
You fade and so fades your picture,
you recover and so does your picture too.
We dig a pit and hide a name
and promise not to speak of it.

Somewhere two people pity each other
in a duel of memory and amnesia.
The relativity of their love and hate
brings in their rhythm a Doppler shift.
Somewhere someone remains silent
and pierces my soul with the noise of it.

21
Telescope

So I buy this incredible telescope.
It brings things closer.
I focus it on the moon
and it comes closer.
I focus it on the stars
and see grandma there.
Then I focus it on you
but you don't come any closer.
So I realise
that the telescope
is not incredible after all,
it is just our eyes.

22
Thereafter

When you released the grip
on my arms
I released my grip
on reality.
Now every night is a blur.
Our unkissed lips come so near
like the twin peaks of a mountain
shrouded in mist.
Behind the cover
do they kiss,
the mountain peaks?
It is so unclear
the mix of reality and dream.
One more cup of memory
I must drink
before the dawn,
else the night won't pass,
it never has been.

23
A Slow Stirring Surface

Boredom and I sit together
looking at the pictures you post
from the hills of Uttarakhand
as freezing frames of stillness.

Boredom and I sit together
trying to feel in a cafe
the warmth of your woolens
in the cold of your cottage.

Boredom and I sit together
trekking a spoon to the rim
to see the fall of sugar
into the lake in the cup.

Boredom and I sit together
blowing a breeze from the breath
before the setting of the lips
into the slow stirring surface.

24
Inconsequentiality

Yes, we met
like an inconsequential
punctuation mark
in a long sentence.
Under the canopy
of your overworked eyes
there was no time
to rest or relax.
The morning sweeper
will sweep aside
my forgotten smile,
your unspoken goodbye.
Except the 'hello' that
stepped from behind
will linger in the hall
for quite a while.
Tonight your eyes
set a bit early,
tonight I claim
my win from destiny.
Tonight my mind waxes
into a new moon,
tonight you dream
of inconsequentiality.

25
A Syntax Error

I do not peep out
of the window
lest the snake of
the day makes an entry.

The chirpings of
the birds enter my room,
early morning,
early memories.

The bug of the world
blights the mind
and the code of life
will not compile.

A gale of silence
uproots the trees,
but the leaves of data
fly nowhere.

26
Rhododendrons

In the country of rhododendrons
I imagined walking with our family.
I imagined taking pictures
of the ancient temples of Baijnath.
I imagined posing at Birthi Falls
and lodging at Munsiyari.
Imagination trekked to Kaliya
and settled at beautiful Chaukori.
At Mukteshwar we fall in love
with the setting sun.
At Naukuchiyatal we get
lost in its serenity.
A short trip to Nainital and
a long stretch of eternity.
Flora and fauna and a bit
of sunshine for company.
See how imagination is
gradually eating me.

27
Silence of the Sleet

What if the world attains dystopia
and we are the last beings alive?
You work on your singularity somewhere,
I on mine somewhere else,
trying to discover each other
over the remnants of ether,
like a blind man trying to see
something beautiful but too far to touch.
We communicate with our devices
that elude from giving our locations,
we crisscross deserts of ice
and sail through seas of sands
as time like drops drip from the clock
while we quest to someday meet,
fully knowing that we are the last beings alive
and the next is the silence of the sleet.

28
The World of Vestigial Organs

The ears of the sky
convalescent in thunder
can't hear your words.

The skin of inhibition
covering the rains
can't feel your touch.

The eyes of electric
coursing in the wind
can't see your face.

The nose of the night
chilling in the air
can't breathe your breath.

The tongue of the
corpulent footpath
can't taste your footsteps.

Love is a cyborg
in a world of organs
turning vestigial.

29
Gift

You gifted me,
a gentle gift,
a song of Gurudev –

Tomaro ashime prano mono loye...
To your infiniteness I bring my heart and mind...

The song travels in my body
and lodges in my being.
Do I deserve it?
How do I let it go?

What do I give you
in return – something
groomed impeccably,
flawlessly made up

or something
unkempt, ruffled
like joy?

30
Morning Peace

Morning flaps its wings
from the turret of snores.

A train of light halts
and spills a glow of souls.

Empty hands of chill
frisk jitters on the skin.

Lost children of sound
are found playing in chirps.

A girl dreams talking
to Derrida in French.

A man calls for peace
after talks of hatred.

If I don't love you much
the world will be much worse.

Acknowledgements

Some of these poems have been published in anthologies like *Converse: Contemporary English Poetry by Indians*, *Toshali Anthology of Poetry*, *Cognitive Slides*, and *Global Poetic Ethos*; in journals like *Shot Glass Journal*, *Masticadores USA*, *Culture and Quest*, *Aloka Magazine*, *Setu Bilingual Journal*, *Saaranga Magazine*, *Medha Journal*, *Kabita Live*, *Borderless Journal*, *The Wagon Magazine*, *Creative Flight*, and *Anansi Archive* (Runner-up poem "Units of Forgetting" in Winter 2023-24 Competition).

I am thankful to my publisher Musca Press for publishing this collection of thirty poems of mine, which is a sequel to my last collection of poems *Etesian::Barahmasi*. I am also thankful to poet Duane Vorhees for introducing me to Musca Press. I am grateful to my dear friend and fellow poet Ananya Chatterjee for all the inspiration. I am also indebted to my family members for their support. Special thanks go to my teachers Mr. Steve Menezes, Prof. Sanjukta Dasgupta and Prof. Malashri Lal for their encouragement. Gratitude also goes to my fellow poets Kushal Poddar and Basudhara Roy, friends at *EKL Review* and the Intercultural Poetry and Performance Library (IPPL) for always being there.

Author Bio

Born in Calcutta of the late 1970s, Amit Shankar Saha is the author of four critically-acclaimed collections of poems, *Balconies of Time* (2017), *Fugitive Words* (2019), *Illicit Poems* (2020) and *Etesian::Barahmasi* (2024). He also has published a non-fiction collection titled *A Portrait of the Artist as a Young Essayist* (2023), an academic book titled *Transitions: Indian Diaspora and Four Women Writers* (2023), and has co-edited a collection of short stories titled *Dynami Zois* (2018).

He is widely published and has won numerous awards, including the Wordweavers Prize, has been nominated for the Pushcart Prize, the Griffin Poetry Prize, and the Best of Net anthology. His poems have been included in anthologies like *World Poetry Yearbook*, *Best Indian Poetry*, the *Yearbook of Indian Poetry in English*, *Converse: Contemporary English Poetry by Indians* and others.

He is the Editor-in-Chief of *EKL Review* and Assistant Secretary of the Intercultural Poetry and Performance Library. He has a PhD in English from Calcutta University and works as Associate Professor and the Head of the Department of English at Seacom Skills University.

His website is amitshankarsaha.com

www.ingramcontent.com/pod-product-compliance
Lightning Source LLC
Chambersburg PA
CBHW060033040426
42333CB00042B/2413